Design & Concepts L.L.C.
December Issue

House of:
Lisabeth Design

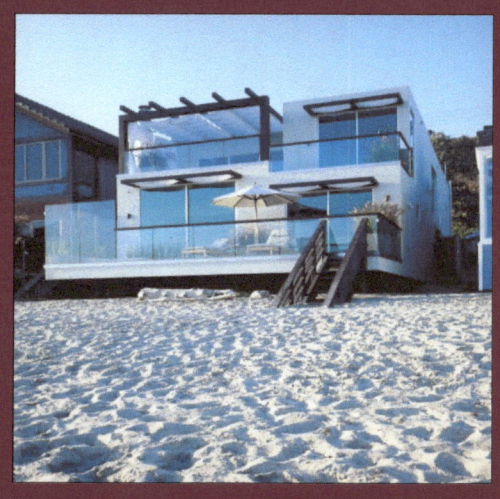

Today's Issue:

- *Doggy's world*
- *Fashion No's*
- *Design or Not*
- *Featured Business*

House of Lisabeth Design 2013

- HEALTH TRENDS
- Summer travel get away
- DOGGY'S WORLD
- THE BUZZ
- FASHION NO OR NOT-FASHION THIS OR FASHION THAT
- NIGHTLIFE
- DESIGN THIS- PERSPECT ENDURE DESIGN
- TRENDY OF 2013-UP TO THE MINUTE 2013
- LIVE EVENTS
- FEATURED BUSINESS: BUSINESS OF- YESTERDAY, -TODAY, AND TOMORROW
- ARIZONA EVENT(S) 4th of July
- POLICTICS TRANSFORMED
- JOKES/COMICS
- FIND US!
- ARIZONA MAP CALENDER

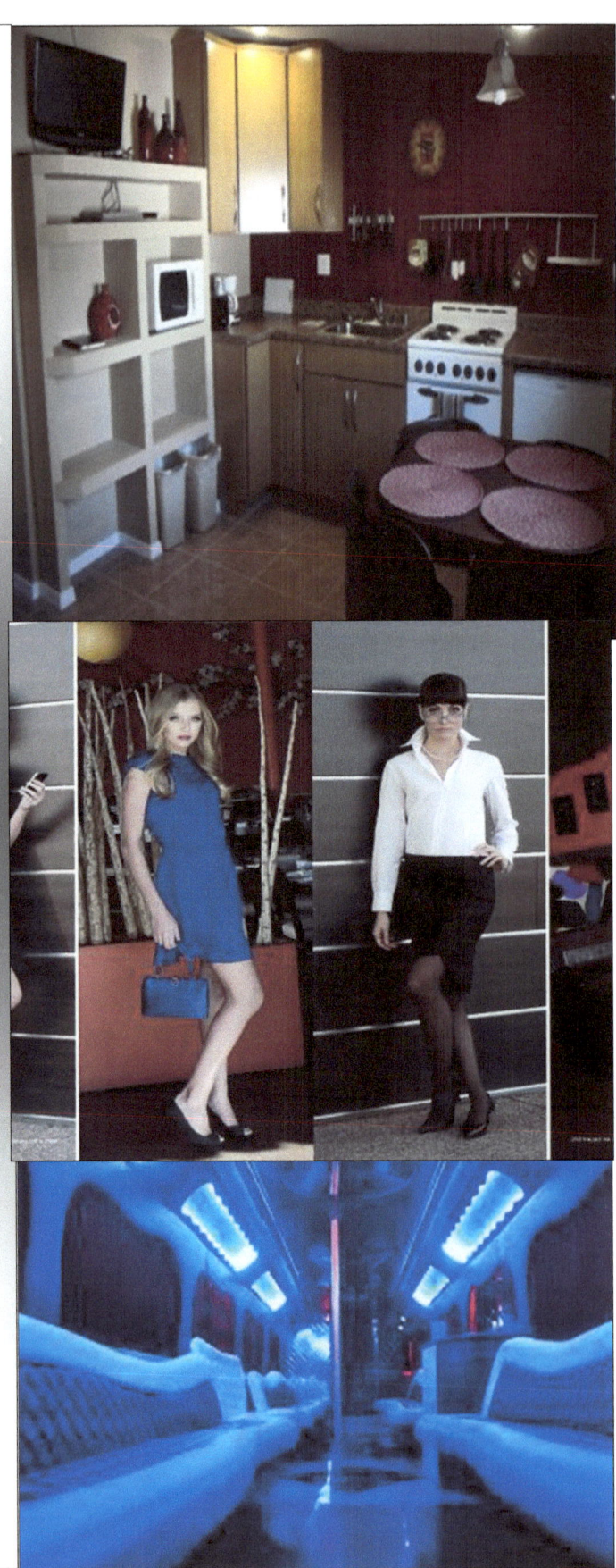

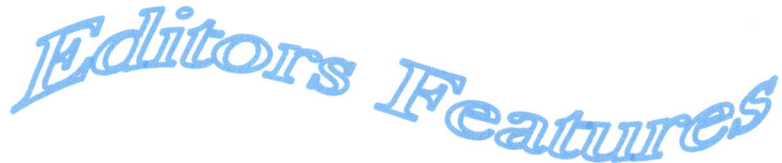

Health Trends

Keeping you colon clean

Colon cancer is cancer of the large intestine (colon), the lower part of your digestive system. Rectal cancer is cancer of the last several inches of the colon. Together, they're often referred to as colorectal cancers.

Most cases of colon cancer begin as small, noncancerous (benign) clumps of cells called adenomatous polyps. Over time some of these polyps become colon cancers.

Polyps may be small and produce few, if any, symptoms. For this reason, doctors recommend regular screening tests to help prevent colon cancer by identifying polyps before they become colon cancer

So how can we prevent colon cancer?

Symptoms range from poor diet to fiber intake. While I was looking up Q and A's I soon came by some concerns about this cancer. One person asked what percentage of people face the risk of colon cancer. Answer was everyone was at risk and especially those with family history and poor diets. That's a concerning look at the cold hard truth. In estimated cases from the United States 2013 statistics it is estimated that there are 102,480 new cases each year and 50,830 of colon and rectal death.

Most of the over the counter medication you see at your local pharmacies can help with preventative and treating. Also fiber and of course healthy eating. Healthy choices effect you for life.

Ways to prevent colon cancer:

- Fiber
- Vitamin D
- don't Hold it (go to the bathroom when you need to)
- Water
- Exercises
- Colonoscopies
- Cleaning your colon

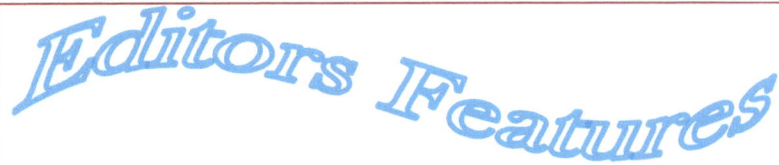

<u>Gymnastics</u>

For those of you who are fans of the Olympics then you have a chance to join in on the fun. The Olympians train for years on there choice of fit field, bicycling, water sports, balance beams etc.
Now you can become a Olympian your self by theses easy steps:

1.) Join a gym
You want to join a gym with the kinds of activities that you want to do. For instance if you were to go online then you can look up your local gyms that provide equipment like balance beams or something similar. I suggest Google, Bing, etc.
2.) Stretch and flexibility is important also, so if you want to take in some flexibility classes like yoga or something similar go ahead.
4.) Also make sure to maintain your healthy diet and exercise program

You'll soon be join in with the Olympians and represent your Country's Colors!

G O U S A !

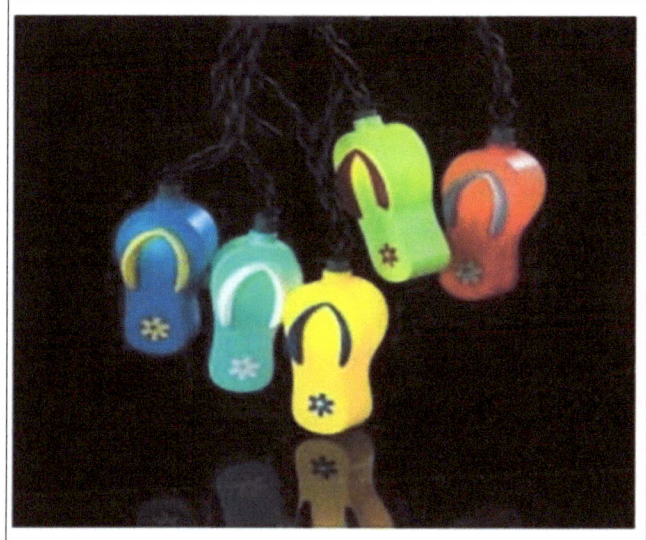

The World of Entertainment

FAVIORTE BOOKS OF THIS MONTH...

Command Authority
Tom Clancy

There's a new strong man in Russia but his rise to power is based on a dark secret hidden decades in the past. The solution to that mystery lies with a most unexpected source, President Jack Ryan.

Robert Ludlum's The Bourne Retribution (Bourne Series 11)

Jason Bourne is one of the most popular and compelling characters in modern fiction. Originally created by bestselling author Robert Ludlum, now New York Times bestselling writer Eric Van Lustbader carries on Ludlum's legacy with a new novel about the rogue secret agent who has lost his memory . . .

The Invention of Wings
Sue Monk Kidd

Writing at the height of her narrative and imaginative gifts, Sue Monk Kidd presents a masterpiece of hope, daring, the quest for freedom, and the desire to have a voice in the world.

Hetty "Handful" Grimke, an urban slave in early nineteenth century Charleston, yearns for life beyond the suffocating walls that enclose her within the wealthy Grimke household. The Grimke's daughter, Sarah, has known from an early age she is meant to do something large in the world, but she is hemmed in by the limits imposed on women.

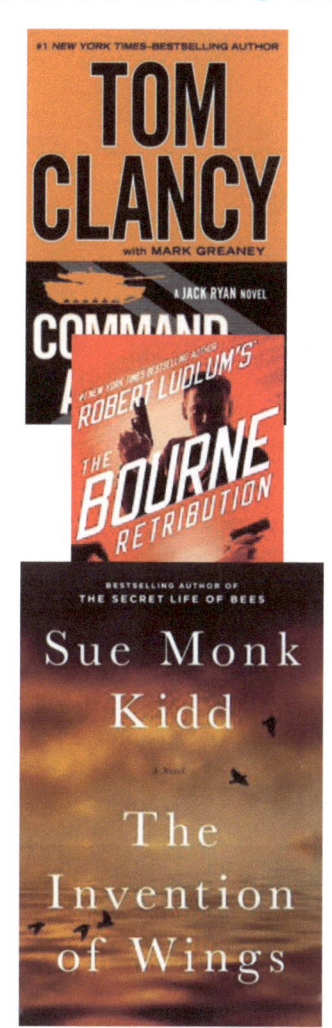

Doggy's World
Music Events:

U.S. Airways Center Presents

Pink
Dec 5th at 7:30
TD Garden, Boston MA

Justin Timberlake
Us Airways , Phoenix AZ
December 2nd 8pm

Jingle Ball with Miley Cyrus ,
Robin Thick, Pitbull and Enrique
Iglesias
Friday December 13,
New York, Madison Square
Garden

201 E Jefferson St. Phoenix,
AZ 85004 602-379-7878

Marquee Theatre Presents!

Margret Cho
December 4 8pm

Artic Monkey
December 9 8pm

Mushroomhead
D E C WITH ONE EYED DOLL,
UNSAIDFATE, IONIA, FATAL
MALADY, SERUM 10
December 10 8pm

1 E Main St. Mesa, AZ
85201 480-644-6501

Fashion No or not....
Brought to you by: Lisabeths Design

The Red Dress

When you see the Red Dress you think elegance, classic and timeless. Yes the red dress is a dress for all occasions. We see everything from the mysterious black to the subtle blue or the out there pink. Yet the Red dress has been the George Clooney of the pack. The one that sits and will never leave your closets or anywhere else. Take for example the ultimate red party. A custom when throwing a ball or raiser or any function for a cause. The most relied on colors would be the black and white balls or the red balls. These types of custom party's are made for elegance and tradition. Bringing old to new. I once saw an red dress event and thought that this has to be one of those blue ribbons types deal were you wear to support. But as you would know the red dress was the show of the show. Different styles and rays coming from all stems all complimenting the Red Dress. The Red color, the Red elegance. A red dress party comes in all shapes and sizes meaning that for each benefit cause or what have you comes the matching of the red dress. So men our not necessary out of the red dress glamor process just asked to match (preferably with a nice tuxedo) Here something to think about..... The Red Dress, was a song made in 2005 for a English girl group Sugar babes from their fourth studio album, Taller in More Ways (2005). The group's members wrote the song in collaboration with its producers, the British songwriting and production team Xenomania, based on the perception that women must expose their body to be noticed "Red Dress" was released in the United Kingdom on 6 March 2006 as the album's third single, and is the first to feature vocals by Amelle Berrabah, following the departure of Mutya Buena in December 2005. The Sugar babes performed a cover of the Arctic Monkey's song "I Bet You Look Good on the Dance floor" as the single's B-side.

SO WHEN YOU GO TO A RED DRESS PARTY OR JUST WANT TO GLAM THINGS UP WITH A RED DRESS THEN YOU THINK OF THE SONG .....

Places to buy .... ------------------

1.) www.modcloth.com
2.) www.simplydresses.com
3.) www.bluefly.com
4.) www.forever21.com
5.) www.anntaylor.com

DESIGN SEO STYLE CREATE SEO LIFE

DONT BUY MEAT

The worthy of the worth and the Elite of the Elite make a common general statement. " DONT BUY MEAT!" You may ask what dose this mean, no meat no nothing don't buy it if its not out there for a good reason or a beneficial reason don't buy it. I once took a seminar on how you can here 100 things at a time and not understand everything that you are listening to. For instance a commercial can advertise the same tactics, like hey we have this new and improve staple, but yet what is going to make you buy this new and improve staple in the first place. Putting away your needs and obvious i just so happened to lose my normal staple. You start to realize that you don't need the automatic closer, the quick throw back metal thing that snaps back faster then any other staple after you squeeze. You just need a super awesome staple. A staple the thing of necessity. So by saying this i again tell you " DONT BUY IT" DONT LOOK AT IT DONT THINK ABOUT IT BECASUE MORE THEN LIKELY YOU ALREADY HAVE IT.

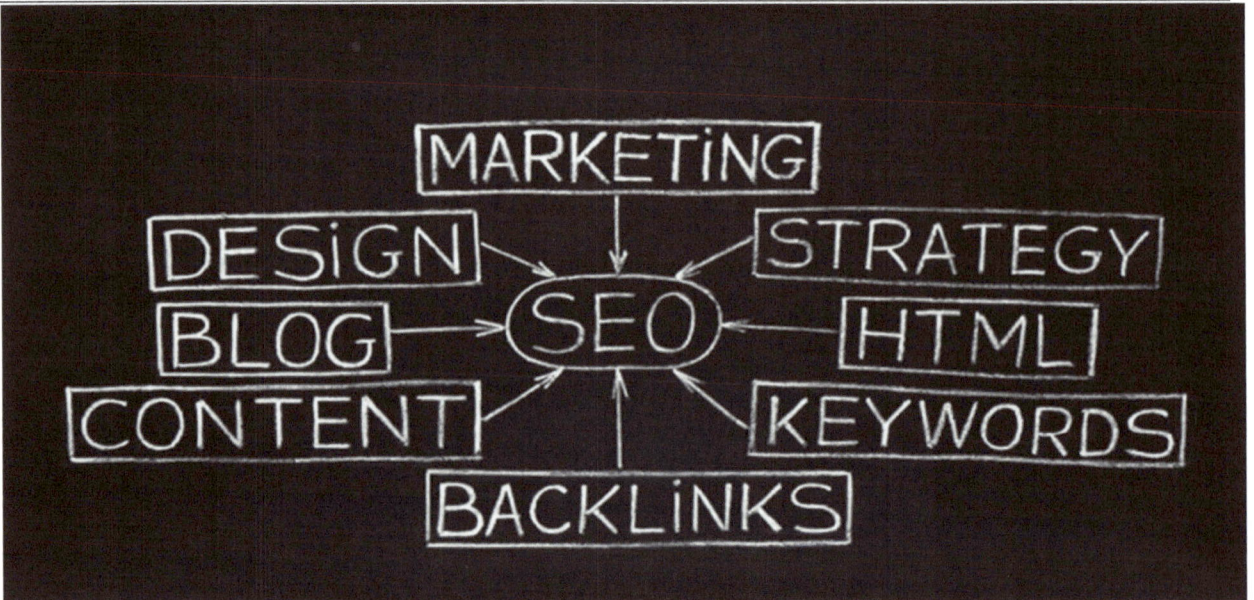

Tom Cruise Wows us in another year!

Its been another exciting years for Tom Cruise with the release of his latest movie to add to his top hitting films , Oblivion we now see a different and new side of him.

As a 14 year old Franciscan seminary student Thomas Cruise Mapother IV, had thought that maybe in the future he wasn't going to be were he is now. We should all hope not, with future projects coming up like Edge of Tomorrow, and Mission Impossible 5 we look forward to another thrilling year with Tom Cruise.

We also see another side coming out of Tom Cruise after his divorce from ex wife Katie Holmes, were he recently divorced in 2012. Latest supporters like ex wife and friend Nicole Kidman were by his side while others from the Hollywood circle helped with encouragement. Latest tweets from Tom's camp show gratitude and thanks from him to his colleagues. We like to see the encouragement from our fellow Tom Cruise fans. With a net worth of 250 million we know that the Tom Cruise Camp will surely show us the worthiness of there movie making epics.

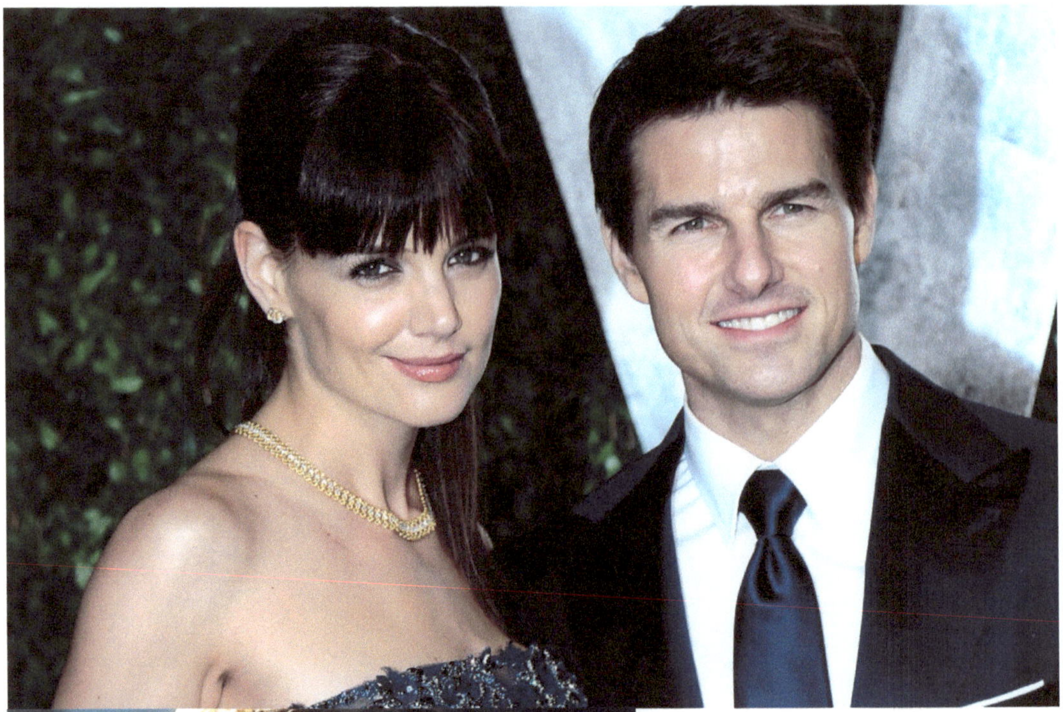

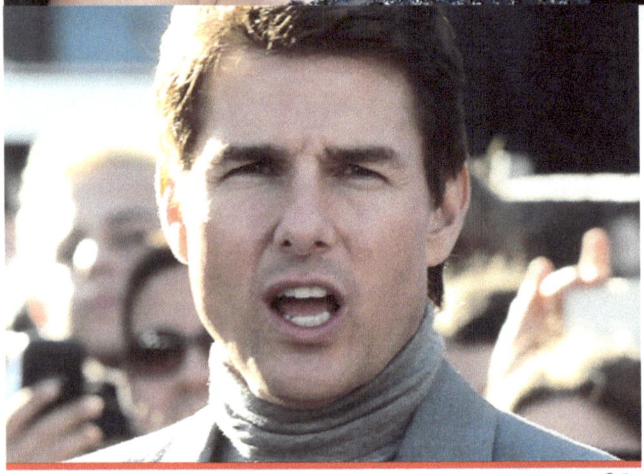

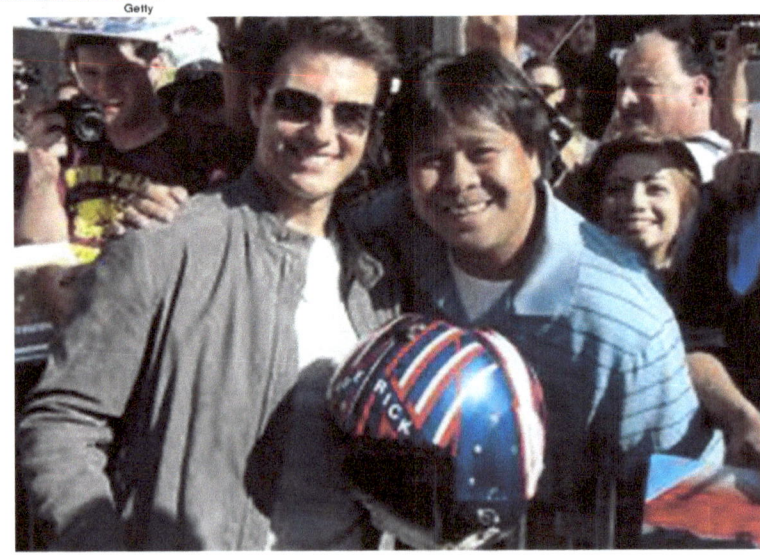

2013 Victoria Secret Fashion Show!

This years fashion show is full of models and more models to show case fashion in high gear!

You can expect anyone from Klum to Alessandro Ambrose to anyone in between. We like to see high fashion sexy lingerie and sexy models to show case not to mention a hot performance by Taylor Swift!

Now how hot can the 2013 Victoria Fashion Show get

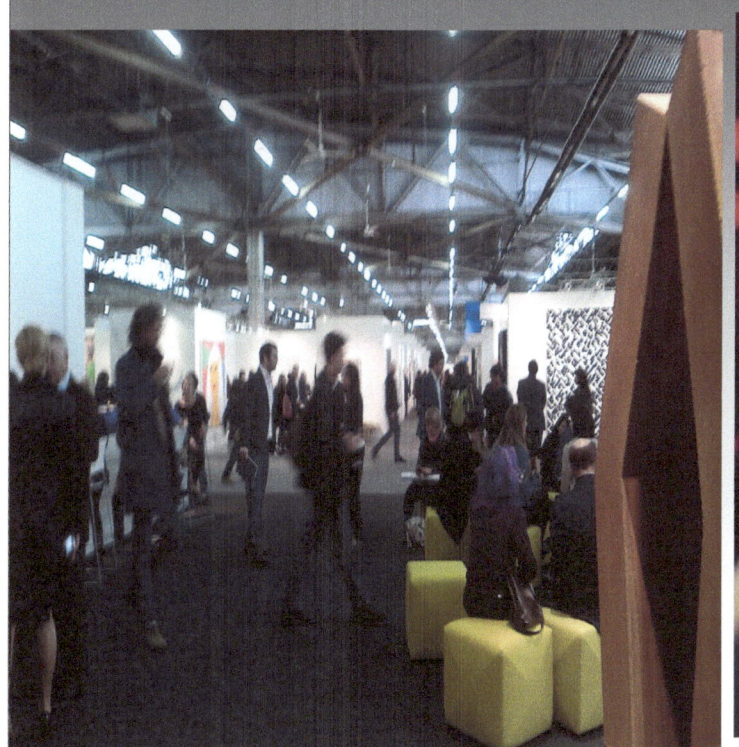

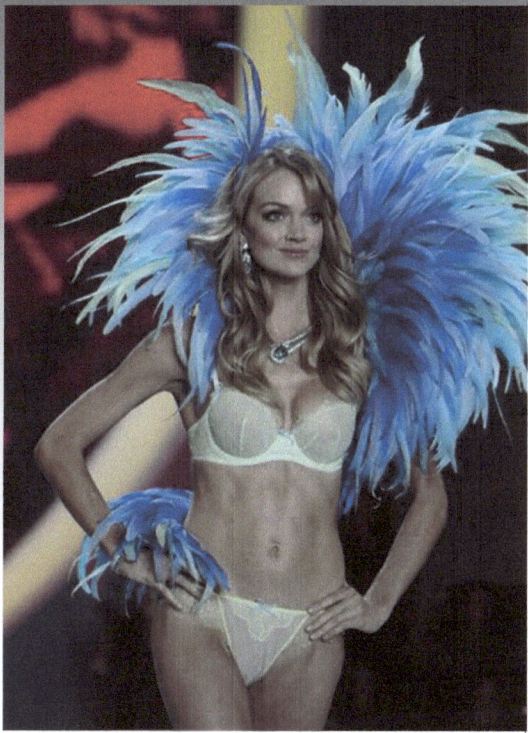

Trendy News What you want to know

Netflix brings back " The Killing" for a sixth episode

Netflix is bringing back the canceled show about a police drama, hint another CSI ...and will be available to its over 50 or so million viewers. Or so… The killing is a murder mystery that Mireille Enos and Joel Kinnaman play Seattle homicide detectives Sarah Linden and Stephen Holder, respectively, in the series, which is based on the Danish drama, Forbrydelsen.

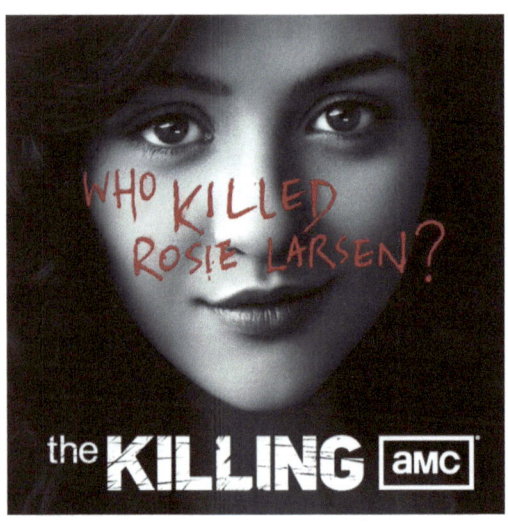

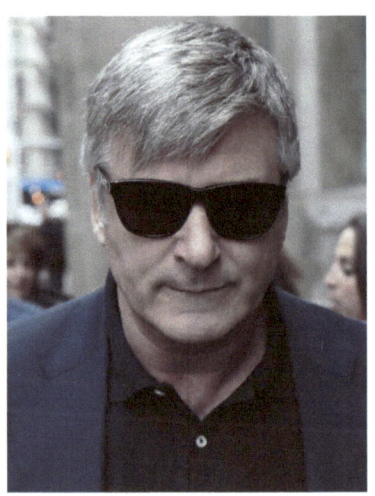

Alec Baldwin and the GAY Slur

Here is the scene Alec Baldwin walking out being ambushed by paparazzi and then out of anger or frustration or both the 55 year old actor yells out " C—-sucking F-g." This on Nov 14 when he was outside his New York City home. Later on getting checked by Anderson Cooper who questions his ethics. He later let out a public apology and said, "What I said and did this week, as I was trying to protect my family, was offensive and

unacceptable. Behavior like this undermines hard-fought rights that I vigorously support." So What we can say is live and learn.

New Technology for the modern geek

3. Best Grills: Philips Avance Taste Infusion

This glorified barbecue lets you infuse your meat with lovely smoke, wine and herb flavors via the reservoirs at the back. Only the middle of the grill has the heat for proper charring, though the edges still come out very tasty.

5. Best Grills: George Foreman Family Grill & Melt

Fat drains smartly into the drip tray on this lean, mean, etc machine, whilst your meat sears beautifully in between scorching hot plates. It's a tad on the small side though – maybe George Foreman's "Family" isn't any too puckish.

.6. Kitchen Aid Artisan

Kitchen Aid makes beautifully designed and highly functional kitchen gadgets, this Artisan toaster is no different; offering a load of quirky options to ensure your toast is the best it can be. There's an automatic sensor which lowers the bread into place, plus an LED countdown timer – for ultimate browning control. An added toastier rack lets you make those gooey, cheesy grilled sandwiches – for when toast just doesn't cut it.

NEW TECHNOLOGY VS THE OTHER GUYS.....

Tech and Tech Gaming the kinds of technology fun we can have that bring our new age kids more up to speed then some of the fastest computers out there. There's really just one thing that's been dominating the tech scene this week, and that's Sony's PlayStation 4. Getting the jump on Microsoft's Xbox, the PS4 launched in the US yesterday and will be available here in a fortnight. Other companies have been busy as well with Google-owned Motorola revealing a brand new handset, the Motorola Moto G. Head to our reviews section to read our thoughts on it, or just glance below for a selection of stories from around the web.

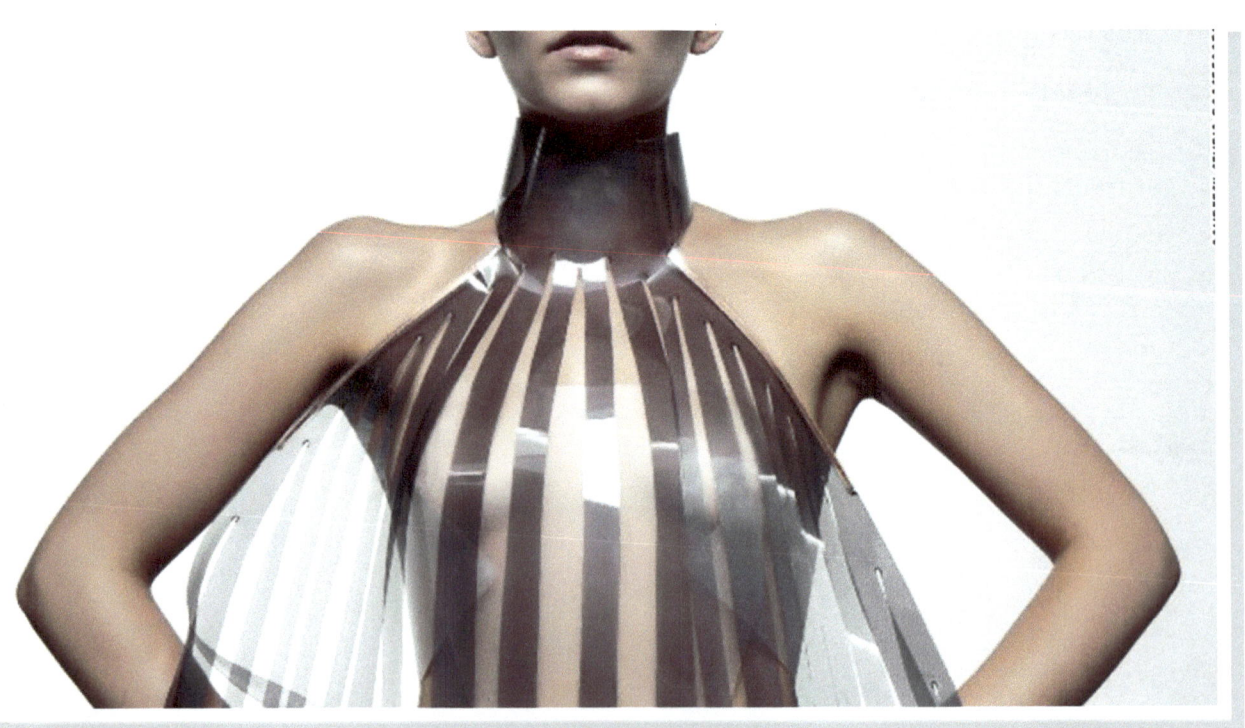

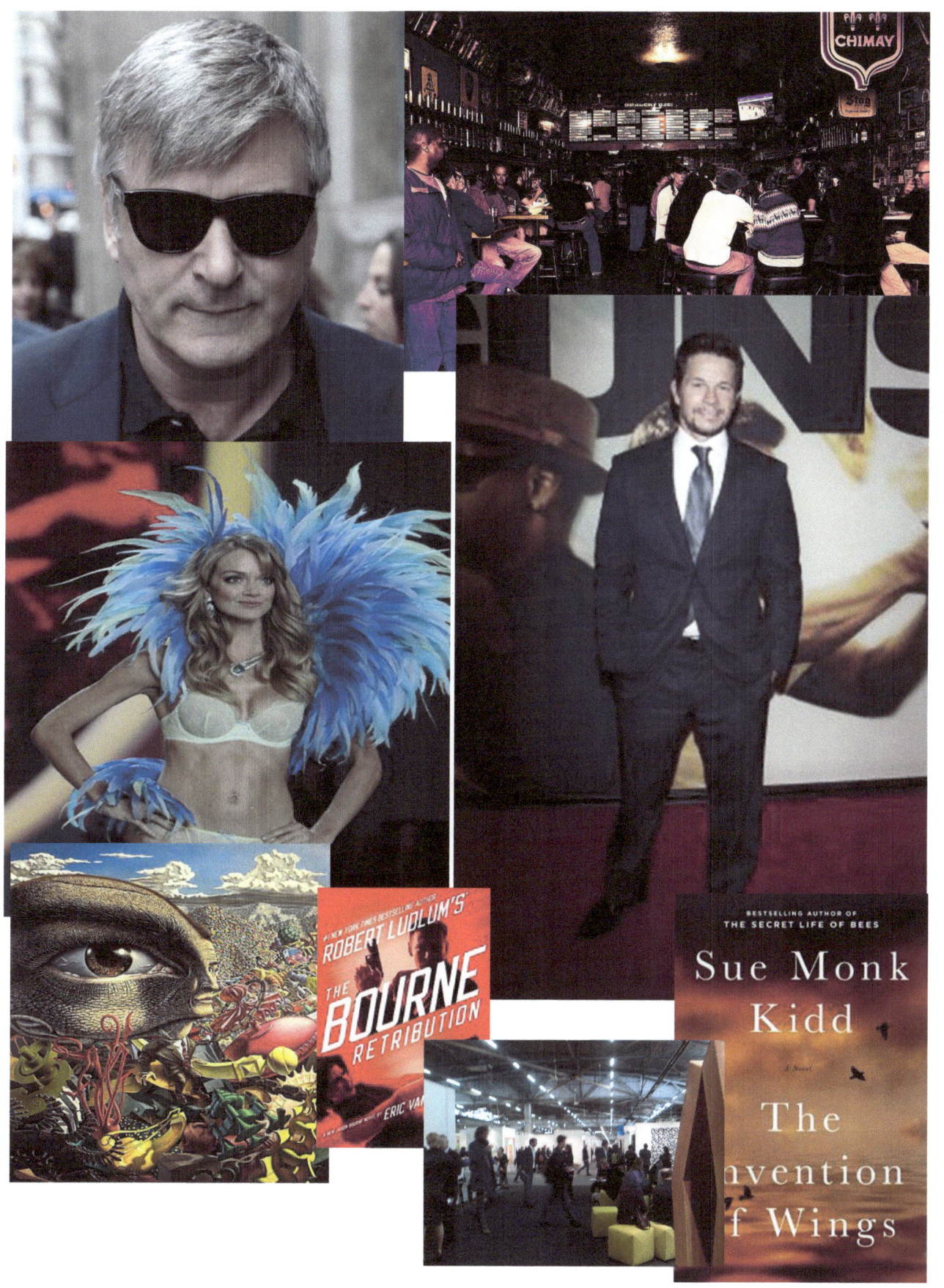

Social apps and more

Find us !

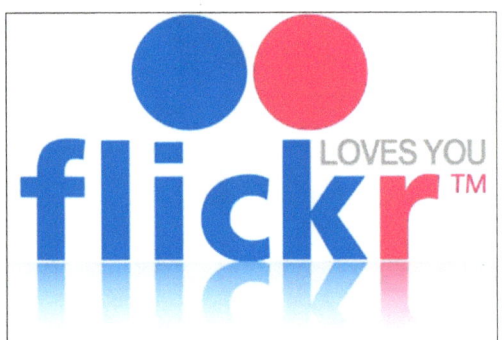

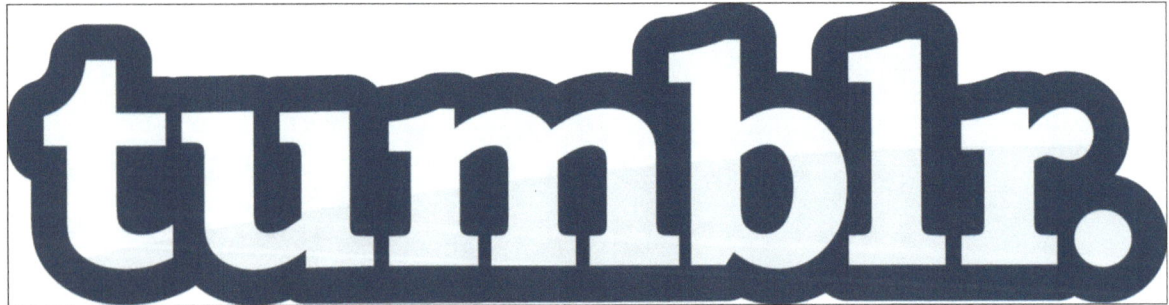

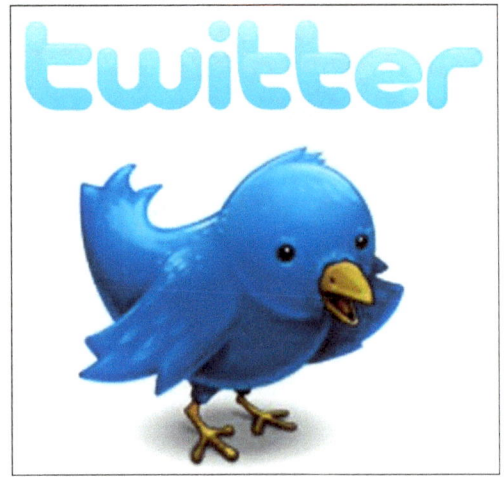

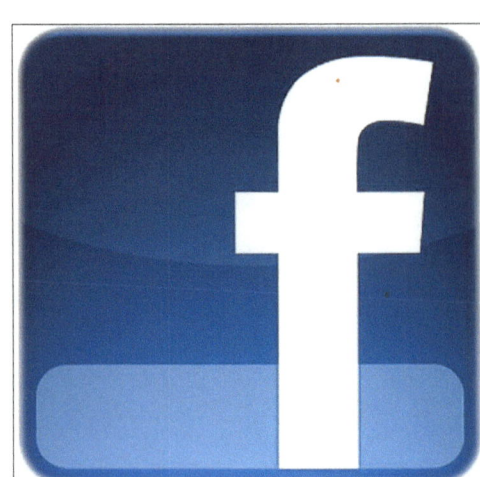

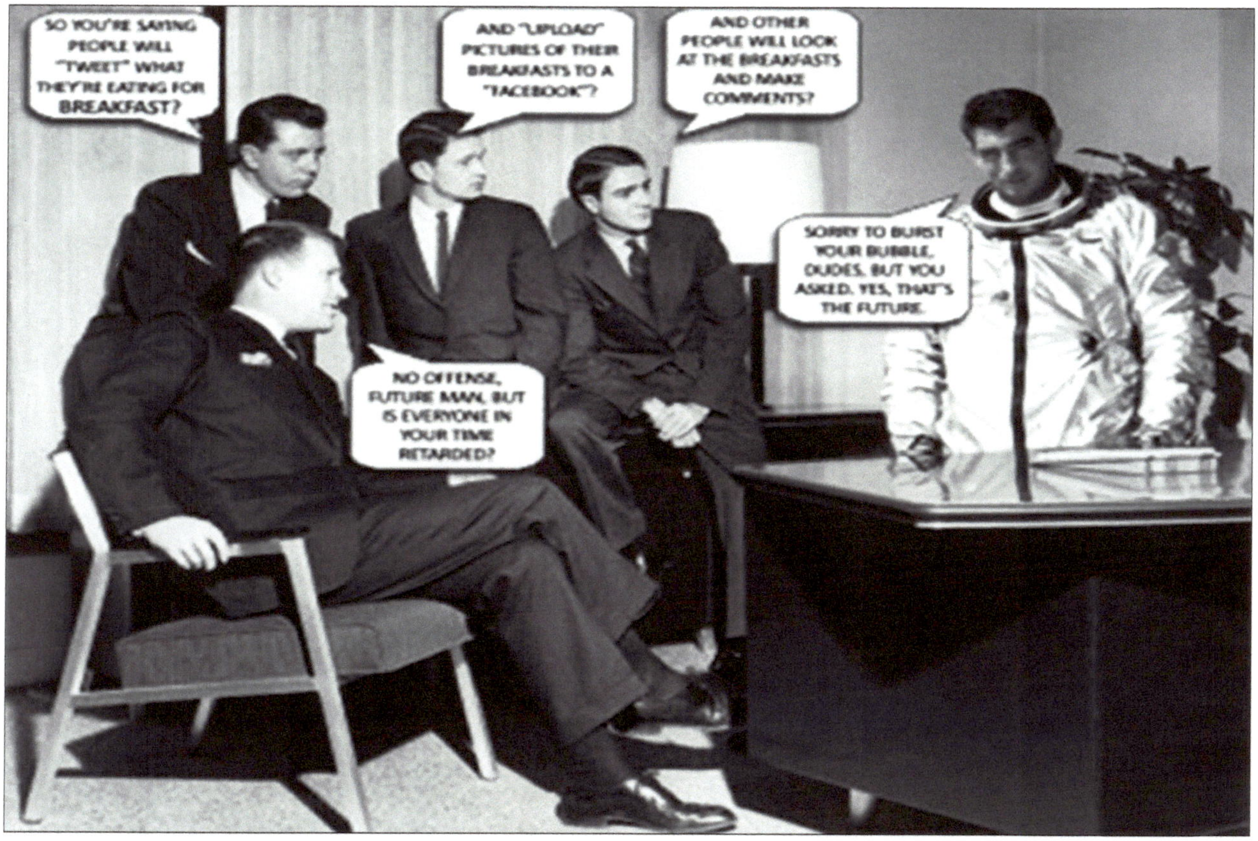

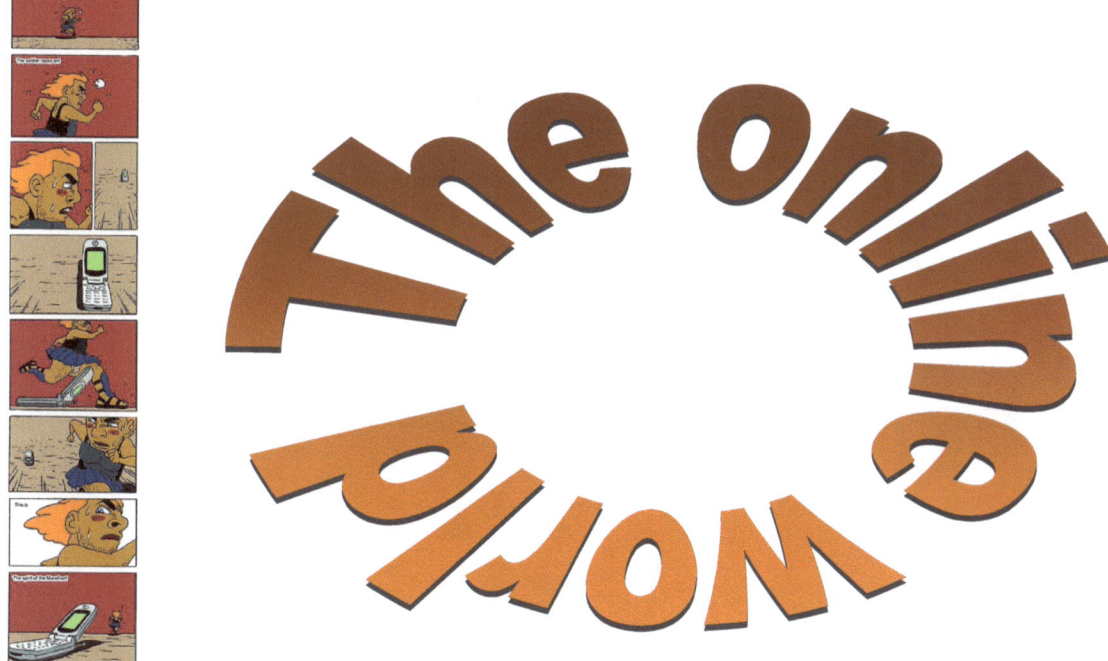

The online world

According to Forbes

Twitter and the IPO

So while now you know that Twitter is officially on the market share list still according to sources say that you can still get a piece of the pie for free.
Twitter's bankers appeared to be low-balling the valuation to insure a traditional tech IPO pop, but even so, the expectations for the total valuation crept higher. $8-$10 billion? Nah, $12 easily. $12B? You're kidding right? $15 at a bare minimum. Finally, the stock floated, ripped higher the first day, and now stands at a valuation of $24 billion. And remember, nobody sold any shares in the IPO.

So what dose this mean for Twitter, well the newest to the stock drama will have its ups and downs. And as for investors now they can take a better look at there Twitter account and say " words are thicker then water" or " the apple never falls to far from the tree."

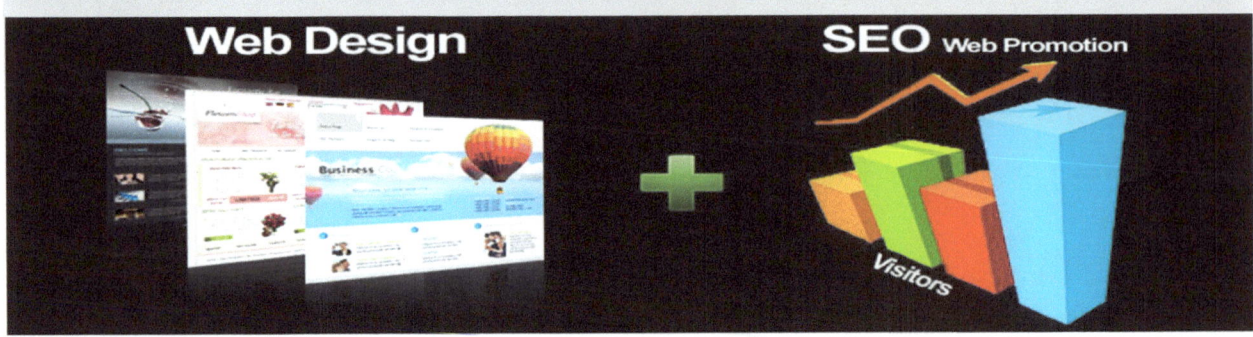

Survive the Realestate market

Don't be Trapped in Real Estate....

Avoid Dual Agency's: Dual Agency occurs when the brokerage firm represents the buyer and seller at the same time

Control business arrangements with title business and services: Title companies that are owned or affiliated with other real estate professionals destroy the integrity of this vital check and balance

Lawyers who sell title coverage: Attorneys cannot negotiate title coverage on behalf of their client when the attorney also represents the title underwriter providing that coverage

Marketing Manipulations that foster Dual Agency's: Many real estate brokerages engage in market manipulations disguised as selling strategies

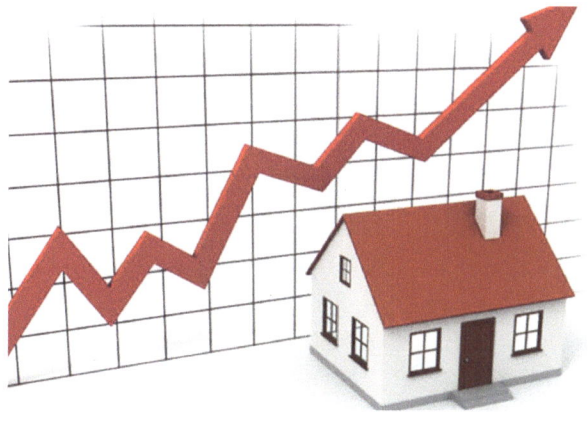

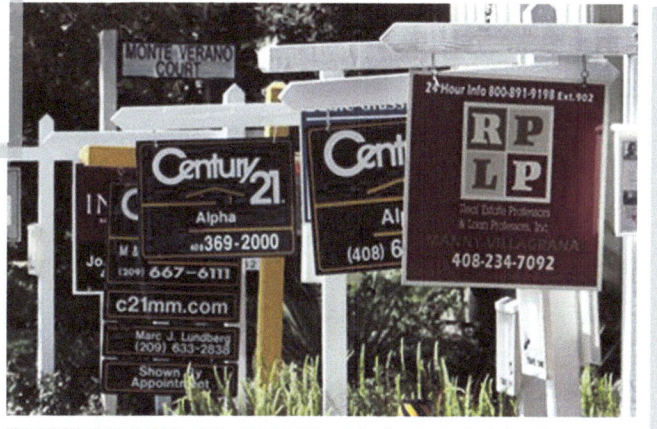

Politics : Special Feature

Obama Health Law updates:

State regulators across the country said they were blindsided by President Obama's decision to change a key health-law provision and spent Friday scrambling to make sense of it. Some said they were unsure whether their state laws would allow them to do what the president suggested.

The president tried to solve a separate issue — his broken promise that people who like their health plans can keep them — by allowing insurance companies to extend health plans that were supposed to be banned.

Toronto's Mayor in trouble

When Mayor Rob Ford was elected in 2010 his questionable history was widely known. Yet voters backed him anyway, eager to shake things up at a City Hall they viewed as elitist and wasteful. Those voters many from Toronto's conservative-leaning outer neighborhoods got their wish, and perhaps more turmoil than they expected.

Now his loyalty is being questioned as he is faced to re signed with questions in regard to a drinking problem, drug use and other off behavior's that is not crowd pleasing. We will see if the future is good or bad whatever it is these behaviors are and can be fixed if the Mayor works to better himself and his campaign.

Syrian Army launches offensives near Lebanon border

Syrian Rebels in the western region on Saturday seam to be ready as they form opposition toward Lebanon as they force hundred to flea the borders. Towns near Qara, Rima and Nabak were said to have the most activity. Lebanon's militant Hezbollah group has deployed thousands of fighters on the Lebanese side of the border in preparation for the battle. With thousands of troops sent and terrorist being killed it was said that the government refers to rebels fighting to overthrow President Bashar Assad as terrorists. More than 120,000 people have been killed so far in the war, now in its third year, according to the Observatory, which closely monitors the violence in Syria through a network of activists across the country. The U.N. said in July that 100,000 Syrians have been killed, and has not updated that figure since. Millions of Syrians have been uprooted from their homes because of the fighting.

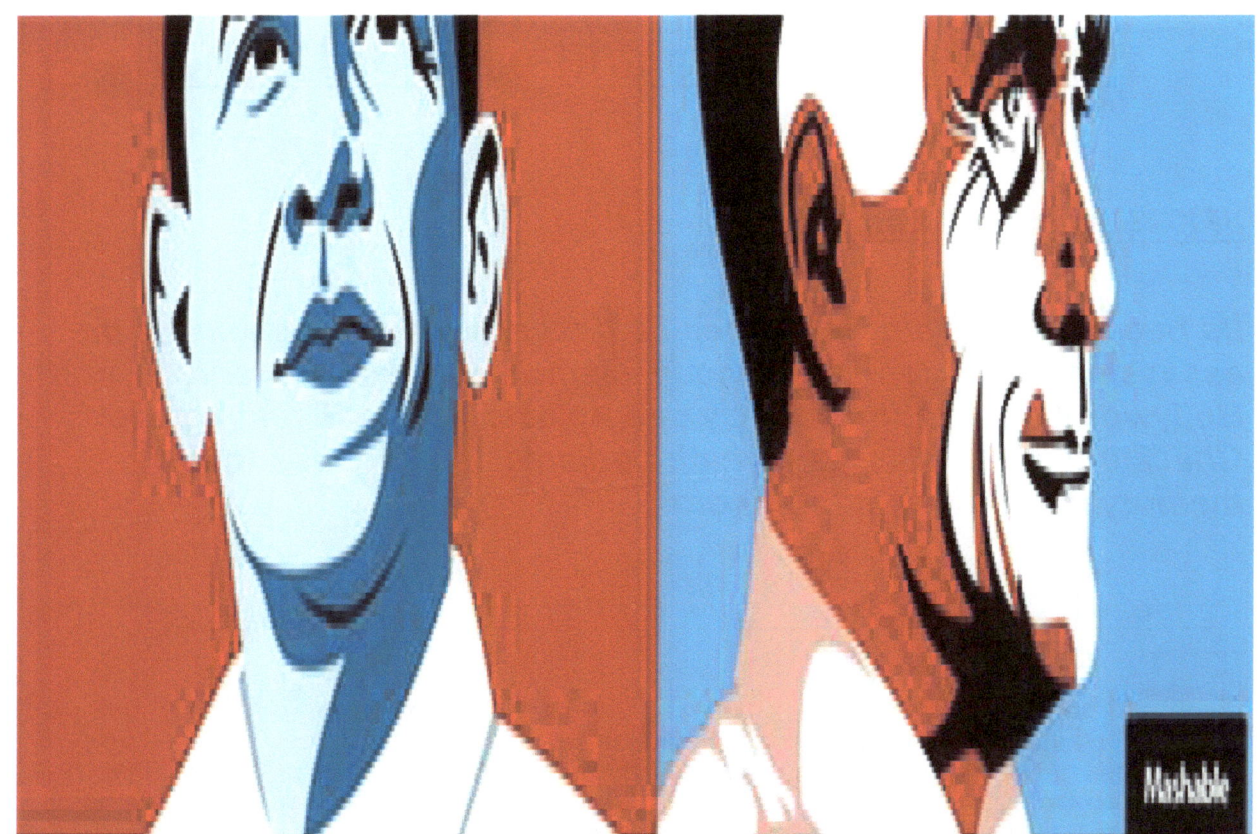

Politics Transformed

THE HIGH TECH BATTLE FOR YOUR VOTE

Politics: The who and what of Politics

JFK– 50 years of memorial

Its been 50 years sin November 22 1963 and we still remember the assassination of John F Kennedy. Memories flash as everyone from Hollywood to all of the country deeply hurt by this divesting event. Check out the JFK library which dedicates its services to his memory. Visit www.jfklibrary.org.

Dallas man gets death sentence for killing a 16-year old babysitter

Death , murder, rape, these are the words you here when you here this story. A Dallas-area man has been sentenced to death for killing his children's baby sitter to silence her in a pending rape case against him. A jury on Saturday condemned Franklin Davis to death for the slaying of 16-year-old Shania Gray. The jury had found him guilty of capital murder Tuesday. He shot and dumped her body in the river because he said that quote her lies ruined his life. This case turned to a capitol murder case were he was officially convicted and waits to be put to death.

Mark Wahlberg argues about actors being compared to Solders

Mark Wahlberg lashed out at actors who equate their jobs to being soldiers in a war, going off on expletive-filled rant during a question-and-answer segment following a Tuesday screening of his film, "Lone Survivor." He was said " For actors to sit there and talk about 'oh I went to SEAL training'? I don't give a f--k what you did. You don't do what these guys did. For somebody to sit there and say my job was as difficult as being in the military? How f--king dare you, while you sit in a makeup chair for two hours," The movie is based on SEAL Team 10's failed attempt to capture a Taliban leader in 2005. It set to be released on Jan. 10, 2014.

DECEMBER 2013

Sunday	Monday	Tuesday	Wednesday	Thursday	Friday	Saturday
1	2	3	4	5	6	7
8	9	10	11	12	13	14
15	16	17	18	19	20	21
22	23	24	25	26	27	28
29	30	31				

November 2013

S	M	T	W	Th	F	Sa
					1	2
3	4	5	6	7	8	9
10	11	12	13	14	15	16
17	18	19	20	21	22	23
24	25	26	27	28	29	30

January 2014

S	M	T	W	Th	F	Sa
			1	2	3	4
5	6	7	8	9	10	11
12	13	14	15	16	17	18
19	20	21	22	23	24	25
26	27	28	29	30	31	

This month will be a great month!

December is like a snow in the wake

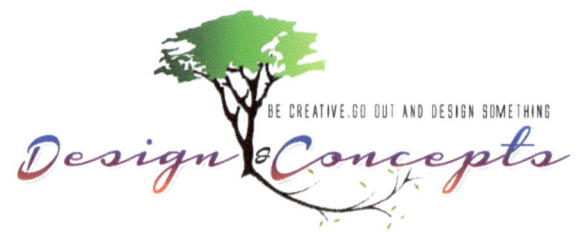

BE CREATIVE.GO OUT AND DESIGN SOMETHING

Design & Concepts

Join our mailing list
and get a free 1
month Subscription
to our magazine!

Owner

Design & Concepts L.L.C
Elizabeth Chavez
602-472-2551
Creativedesignconcepts@rocketmail.com

Place orders by email or contact

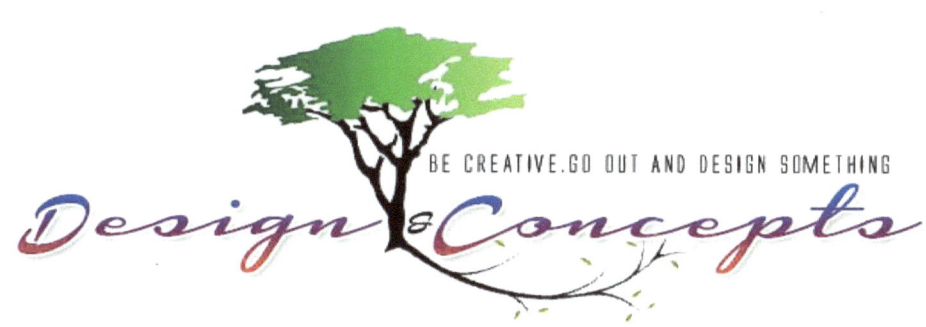

BE CREATIVE.GO OUT AND DESIGN SOMETHING

Design & Concepts

House of Lisabeths Design Magazine
We were started in 2013 as an independent magazine. Our focus is fashion, health and business. We pride ourselves in the design and diversity we offer.
Exclusivity
Our focus is fashion , health and business. Our fashion section includes tips and trends from all over! We also have a online blog that gets tons of clicks per day, check us out online at ......
Our business section is used for local or national business to place a Ad or listing of them selfs. We have total exclusivity In that they connect with not only our magazine but all of our networks simultaneously.
Our hope is to reach across the world along with Water 4 Kids International.
We plan to donate proceeds to this foundation. Our hope is to provide safe water for east Africa.
Check us out on line, Facebook, Twitter, Tumblr, Amazon, and our affiliates websites like Design & Concepts.

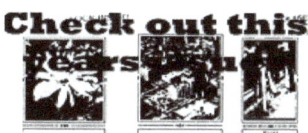

Check out this

Subscriptions:

Get a One– Year subscription for $ 35.00——

Get a two-year subscription for $ 44.95——

Payment Enclosed———— ☐
Charge my credit card—— ☐
Bill me later———— ☐

Send to
Liz Chavez
32 E Ruth ave suite 304
Phoenix AZ 85020
We also take check ,cash, and money orders
Remember when you purchase a subscription you get a
free T– Shirt from Lisabeths Design
Available in men and women
Let us know what you prefer!

Personal Info

Credit
Card#_____
_____
Exp date_____
Signa-
ture_____
Name_____
_____
Ad-
dress_____
_____
City, state ,
zip_____
_____

Also check out our web-site for more info:

Www.designandconcepts.net

Also with your Subscription get a FREE LISABETHS DESIGN T SHIRT

AVAILABLE FOR MEN AND WOMEN

Design and Concepts Blog
Check us out!

http://design-and-concepts.blogspot.com/

Whether its design or consult we strive for newest technology to help get the best for our customers. This means uses the lasted communication interfaces such as blogging, or designated group chat a ears, theses kinds of interactions is what singles out our product and gives it the spot light.
So now we are looking into the future, what dose design have as an impact in our business. Can we expand in a ears like media pamphlets, custom web design, office interior, marketing. These. New technology is what we are leading into.

Media pamphlets is a necessary tool for any business to explain there business to one another. One of our specialties is print and digital design content. We want to match your print media as well as match your online content.

Custom web design is another common but necessary design aspect that we deal with. In web content it's a more free form of design you have More avenues to cover and more space to use. We want this easy connection between you your business card and your web site. At a eyes stand point the design of web is vital in easy access, easy communication and understanding of products. This makes for a marketable place of business.

Office interior is our newest wave we want to help design the basics from chairs to design setting, placing pamphlets and materials in your office for more exposure . Our newest phrase is elegance, and modern design. We look for complimentary and efficiency.

Business

A **business** (also known as **enterprise** or **firm**) is an organization involved in the trade of goods, services, or both to consumers.[1] Businesses are predominant in capitalist economies, where most of them are privately owned and administered to provide service to customers for profit. Businesses may also be not-for-profit or state-owned. A business owned by multiple individuals may be referred to as a company, although that term also has a more precise meaning.

The etymology of "business" relates to the state of being busy either as an individual or society, as a whole, doing commercially viable and profitable work. The term "business" has at least three usages, depending on the scope — the singular usage to mean a particular organization; the generalized usage to refer to a particular market sector, "the music business" and compound forms such as agribusiness; and the broadest meaning, which encompasses all activity by the community of suppliers of goods and services. However, the exact definition of business, like much else in the philosophy of business, is a matter of

www.ingramcontent.com/pod-product-compliance
Lightning Source LLC
Chambersburg PA
CBHW050428180526
45159CB00005B/2456